The Christmas Message

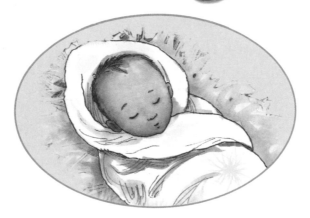

The Savior's birth

Luke 1:26–56, Matthew 1:18–25,
Luke 2:1–20 for children

Claire Miller
Illustrated by Michelle Dorenkamp

CONCORDIA PUBLISHING HOUSE · SAINT LOUIS

At Christmas God sent angels as
His messengers on earth
To tell the news that His own Son
Would have a special birth.

The first to come was Gabriel,
The angel whom God chose
To visit Mary. What a shock!
She stared at him and froze.

"Don't be afraid," the angel said.
"Have I got news for you.
Of all the women in the world,
God's chosen you. It's true!

"You'll have a baby boy, God's Son,
You'll name Him Jesus, and
He'll be the Savior of the world.
He'll come as God has planned."

But Mary didn't understand
How she could have God's child,
So Gabriel explained some more.
He spoke again and smiled.

"The Holy Spirit will come down;
God's power will rest on you.
His holy Son will be your child.
There's nothing God can't do."

How happy Mary was that day.
She sang a thankful song. . . .
An angel came to Joseph next
And said, "You can't go wrong

"By taking Mary as your wife.
Her child will make you glad!
He'll be God's Son, but you can be
His loving, earthly dad."

The news left Joseph so amazed—
God's mom would be his wife!
The Savior he'd been waiting for
Would come into his life!

An angel next appeared at night
To shepherds guarding sheep
Out in a field near Bethlehem,
While most folks were asleep.

A dazzling light flashed in the sky.
An angel came in sight.
The shepherds looked and shook with fear.
Their eyes were wide with fright.

"Don't be afraid," the angel said.
"My news will bring great joy.
Your Savior has been born today—
A holy baby boy.

"You'll find Him in a manger, and
He's lying in some hay.
The stable is in Bethlehem,
Not very far away."

Then angels filled the sky above.
They sang of peace on earth,
And praised the Lord for all He'd done
And for the Savior's birth.

The shepherds rushed to Jesus' side.
They worshiped Him, and told
The angels' wondrous message to
All people—young and old.

God's angels came as messengers
At Christmas—what a sight!
Although we cannot see them now,
They guard us day and night.

So thank God for His precious Son
And angels that are strong.
They cheered the world with news from God
In their most glorious song.

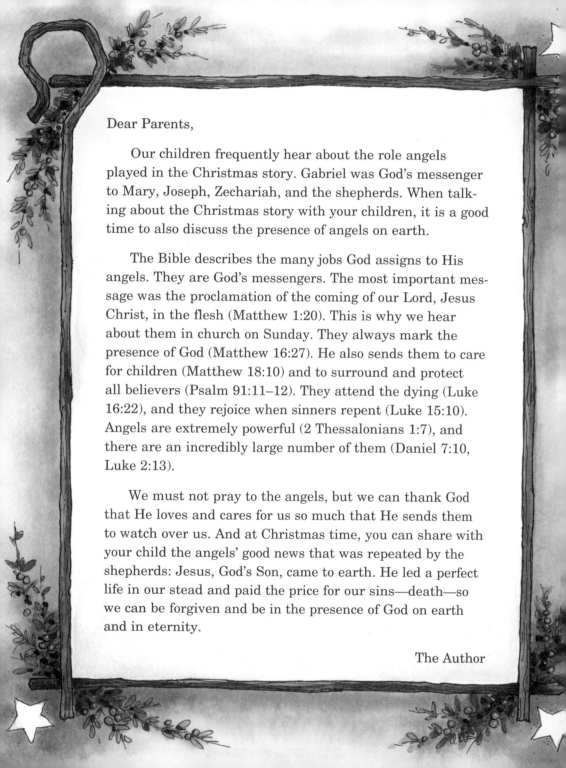

Dear Parents,

Our children frequently hear about the role angels played in the Christmas story. Gabriel was God's messenger to Mary, Joseph, Zechariah, and the shepherds. When talking about the Christmas story with your children, it is a good time to also discuss the presence of angels on earth.

The Bible describes the many jobs God assigns to His angels. They are God's messengers. The most important message was the proclamation of the coming of our Lord, Jesus Christ, in the flesh (Matthew 1:20). This is why we hear about them in church on Sunday. They always mark the presence of God (Matthew 16:27). He also sends them to care for children (Matthew 18:10) and to surround and protect all believers (Psalm 91:11–12). They attend the dying (Luke 16:22), and they rejoice when sinners repent (Luke 15:10). Angels are extremely powerful (2 Thessalonians 1:7), and there are an incredibly large number of them (Daniel 7:10, Luke 2:13).

We must not pray to the angels, but we can thank God that He loves and cares for us so much that He sends them to watch over us. And at Christmas time, you can share with your child the angels' good news that was repeated by the shepherds: Jesus, God's Son, came to earth. He led a perfect life in our stead and paid the price for our sins—death—so we can be forgiven and be in the presence of God on earth and in eternity.

The Author